Garfield
Weighs in!

BY: JiM DAViS

ЯR
Ravette London

This edition first published by
Ravette Limited 1986

Printed and bound in Great Britain
for Ravette Limited,
12 Star Road, Partridge Green,
Horsham, Sussex RH13 8RA
by William Clowes Limited, Beccles and London.

ISBN 0 948456 16 7

Weighs in!

Garfield loves to throw his weight around and he certainly has enough artillary to do so. Enjoy a feast of gags as you watch Garfield heavy the scales of injustice in typical light hearted fashion!